Ferret Dreams

Crittertude

Volume 3

Ferret Dreams: Crittertude, Volume 3

© 2012 David Martin. All rights reserved.

No part of this book may be used or reproduced in any manner whatsoever without written permission except in the case of reprints in the context of reviews. For information, contact **info@crittertude.com**

ISBN-13: 978-0615680743

ISBN-10: 0615680747

Visit Mady and the Gang at **crittertude.com**

[Editor's Note]

When you're young, you're raised to expect the best out of life. As we grow into adulthood, you anticipate the challenges that life unfolds before you. And, at some point, you realize that life often involves elements entirely outside of our control; both pulling at our heartstrings and bringing a tear to our eye. So it is with Crittertude.

We've had a lot of unexpected events happen over the last several years. Back in 2010, we lost our beloved European Starling ("One of Six") to an unknown illness. Late last year, we had to face the unexpected death of Mady the Squiggly Ferret after being blessed by his presence for just over seven years. Never had we thought that we'd have as much difficulty coming to terms with these events as we, in actuality, did.

Would we have changed events, given the ability to travel back in time and fiddle with history? Not by a long shot. The amazing love given by a pet can never be isolated from their ultimate loss. The chance to relish in the love of these unique animals that have so touched our lives not only make us sad and nostalgic; they make us better people for having embraced them in our hearts. And best of all, we're able to re-learn the lessons of unconditional and innocent love, something often forgotten during our youth.

This is our main reason for the ongoing publication of our online comic, Crittertude. We do it not only for the memories of our experiences; we do it (as we've been amazed to learn) also as a result of how much they've touched the lives of their fans across the globe.

This is our passion, and this is their legacy.

David & Susan Martin
August, 2012

Powered by Bioweasel

CRITTERTUDE VOLUME 3

FERRET DREAMS

FERRET DREAMS

FERRET DREAMS

FERRET DREAMS

FERRET DREAMS

FERRET DREAMS

FERRET DREAMS

FERRET DREAMS

FERRET DREAMS

FERRET DREAMS

FERRET DREAMS

FERRET DREAMS

FERRET DREAMS

FERRET DREAMS

FERRET DREAMS

FERRET DREAMS

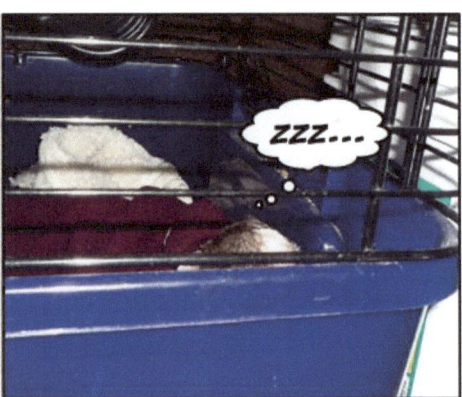

FERRET DREAMS

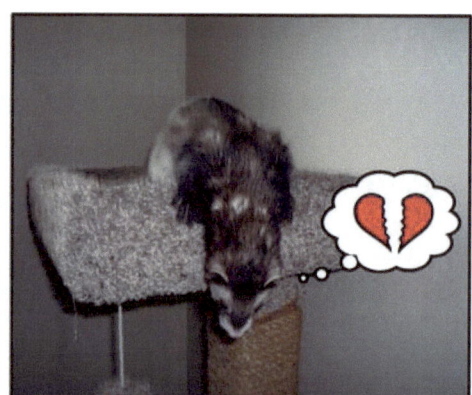

FERRET DREAMS

FERRET DREAMS

FERRET DREAMS

FERRET DREAMS

FERRET DREAMS

FERRET DREAMS

FERRET DREAMS

FERRET DREAMS

FERRET DREAMS

FERRET DREAMS

FERRET DREAMS

FERRET DREAMS

FERRET DREAMS

FERRET DREAMS

FERRET DREAMS

FERRET DREAMS

FERRET DREAMS

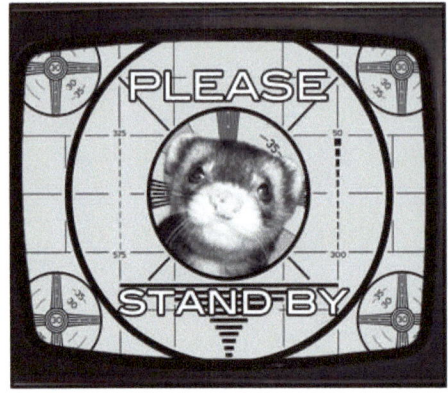

CRITTERTUDE VOLUME 3

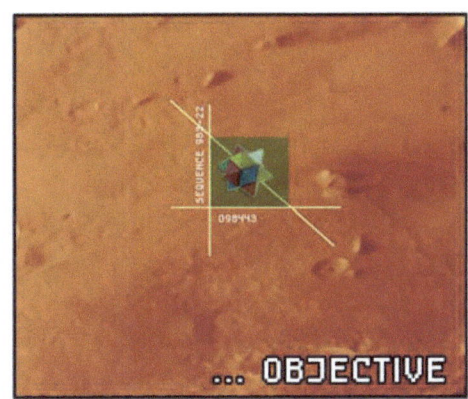
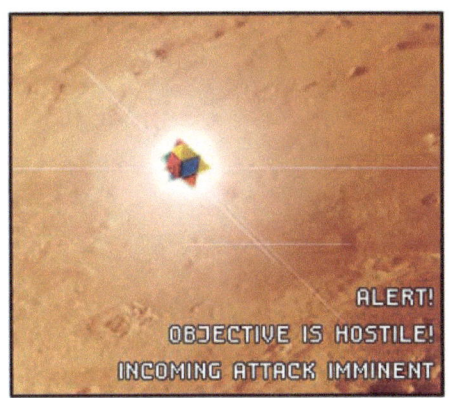

FERRET DREAMS

FERRET DREAMS

FERRET DREAMS

FERRET DREAMS

FERRET DREAMS

FERRET DREAMS

FERRET DREAMS

FERRET DREAMS

FERRET DREAMS

FERRET DREAMS

FERRET DREAMS

FERRET DREAMS

FERRET DREAMS

FERRET DREAMS

www.ingramcontent.com/pod-product-compliance
Lightning Source LLC
Chambersburg PA
CBHW042000150426
43194CB00002B/71